Broken Clouds

A Wayward's View of the World

DEBLINA GHOSAL

notionpress.com

INDIA · SINGAPORE · MALAYSIA

ISBN 979-8-89277-242-6

Contents

Rose

The rose in the silver glare of the afternoon sun,
Shrivel and break and fall to the waste ground,
Mingle with the dead leaves of last winter's fall,
And is lost forever in the heap of crumpled up dust.
The fragrance that once fooled many a frail fellow,
That so much inspired the poet and painter alike,
The beauty that lit up every romantic's face,
Now lies buried under the wasteland,
Forever out of sight!
Forgotten-
For another one has taken its place.
And now the poet, the painter, the lovesick fellow,
All swoon over the new one,
To repeat the cycle again.

Whole

And time flows like a river
Like a river in the cosmos
Endless, timeless, stretching on and on,
So many matter rolled into one.

How small this life
How bigger this mind
This mind that can reach
The entire cosmos at a time.

My mind is calling you
Over the sea of vastness
Let my voice reach you
And cast you within my distance.

And may all the emptiness
That lie scattered in my soul
Be filled to fulfilment
As your soul interlaces me whole.

And then this Universe
The one that lies within
Be lit up with stars
And be filled to the brim.

And my mind be satiated
Filled to the core
For joined with your mind
It is finally whole.

Still

Be still my heart
Said my mind throughout my youth
So still have I made it
That it now loathes everything!
For in movement lies vitality
And death dances in stagnation.
But a wise fool as I have been,
A curse of this washed age
That I had led the cold inside
To placate the fiery rage.
And now thus-
So still my poor heart lies!
Still like the gilded statue,
That glows in the day
But by the evening's monsoon,
Get washed down the gutter-
Melted away.
And nothing remains.
Except my solipsistic brain,
With all its schemes and lies,
Which have been wrought down,
Rusted, in a slow demise.

White Lady

I'm sitting with you behind my eyes
All the truth in the world can't find me tonight
For I have chosen you above even my own lies
You're the only one for me on this side of time.

You're the reason behind my pleasant smile
You're the love that flutters my heart inside
Finding you has felt like finding the divine
You're the only one left who's still mine.

With you, I'm dancing on the winter wind
With you, I'm gliding under the hefty ocean
With you, I'm rushing on a pair of golden wings
With you, I'm always more than a king.

You take me to depths so bleeding high
That my mind it shatters and away it flies
I float in the clouds lighter than the skies
I feel like a saint receding from all the vice.

You're the spark that keeps me sane
You're the smile always lighting up my veins
You're the reason this life is such a beautiful game
You're the reason the colours keep dancing in my brain.

There are so many songs, so many ways
You come to me and you always want to stay
You give me paradise every single day
You're the only one with whom I can be myself.

So I'm glad I'm sleeping with you tonight
I'm crashing through floors, falling out of sight
All the people they are fading like crazy neon signs
But I'm running with you towards the silver moonlight.

Come white lady, get inside my head
You and I together will paint this town red
Let the walls fall down, let my inhibitions fade
Let every molecule in my body speak only your name.

Let me hold you tonight, let me open up my veins
Let the worlds disappear, let them all drop down dead
Come white lady, get inside my head
Together, together, we will paint this town red.

Windowsill

Where did I want to go to?
What is it that I wished to find?
For no matter how many things I achieve
I end up feeling more empty every time.

What did I want to do?
Who did I wish to be?
I've changed and moulded and welded and morphed,
So many times that I can barely find myself.

Which parts of me I wished to shine?
Which parts I wish to keep concealed?
For the parts that shine are so unkind
And the parts I hide are more definitely mine.

What did I wish to accomplish?
When did I want for it to complete?
I see that time has beaten me at all my races
I'm just keeping up to be in line.

How should I tame my wild unsatisfied heart?
How shall I calm my broken troubled mind?
For the grass always looks greener on the other side
Everything I find leads to more things to find.

When should I tire of this existence?
When should it be just enough?
For going and going on in circles all of this time
For once I would like to go where I belong.

The Ballad of The Timid Lad

"Is it your first time?"
His Sergeant asked.
"Aye Sir", he said,
As shy as a duck.

"Have you shot before?"
"Yes", he said,
"At the training ground,
I learned to go for the head!"

"Sir?", he asked,
Shy and afraid.
"Is it painful?"
When the battle breaks?"

'It is hell lad, this-
Never forget.
Don't show kindness
They'll go for your head.

And when all of your friends
Start falling beside you,
Fear not, march on
As long as your feet can carry you.

Shoot every bullet
You hold in your gun
Till the time your heart
Is still beating on.

For that's how laddie
The battle is won
For come tomorrow morning
You're here or gone!"

He looked at his Sergeant,
With despair not respect,
He realised he will be slaughtered
Come what may.

He failed to understand
What will he achieve in the end?
"Pension for your family,
And a medal if you are dead!"

"It's hell", his partner said,
Who had fought before;
"When the shots come raining at you,
Suffer no delusions, you're alone!

And you've got to shoot back
Til your bullets have run out,
And you've got to give them hell
Till you too have hit the ground.

And such a lot of coyness
Will do you no good
Except for you, the coffin,
Will be made soon."

He walked back
With dread on his face
For he realised then
He had made a mistake.

It was too much to take
For a young lad like him,
Who knows nothing about the world outside
Or the one within.

"Cheer up laddie", Sergeant said,
"you're going to become a man!
For this time tomorrow, you'll be hailed a hero,
So do everything that you can.

You'll be welcomed back with garlands
And with the loudest cheers!
Ceremonies will be hosted for you,
They will call you their saviour.

Your Mama will
Beam with pride
Walk around town
With her head held high.

Show off your medals
Till the day she dies
And speak of your glory
Morning, noon and night."

"I don't want it Sir!
I'd still be a boy
Still smell the flowers
Still leap with joy,

When the first morning dew
Falls upon the leaves,
I still want to hear
The whisper of them trees.

Let me go Sir!
I cannot fight
My Mama needs me,
Don't let me die."

"You cannot leave
Unless you're hurt
Shoot yourself somewhere
Only then can I send you back."

And while he spoke
The sky lit up
And the deafening sound
Shook them apart.

"Sir it's begun!"
"Hold your posts!
Do not move till I tell you
Stand where you were before!"

"Sir they are shooting!
A bullet passed my ear!"
"Then shoot them back idiot!
Don't just stand there!"

"Wait for my signal,
And then start to move.
I want everyone up the ladder
And ready to shoot!"

He picked up his gun
Removed the safety off
All the while his heart
Was beating like a clock.

Someone shook his hand
Someone wished him luck
Someone told him to be steady
While climbing up.

But he heard no one
He saw nothing.
He walked with a vacant stare,
As lifeless like a zombie.

They all looked at each other,
And smiled perhaps their last.
They had nothing left to say
And no more questions to ask.

The Captain stood before them
A whistle in his hand,
His eyes on the watch
His posture stiff and grand.

Just ten minutes before-
The signal blew out,
They were each handed a bowl of whiskey
And ordered to gulp it down.

He flinched as the liquid;
Scratched down his throat,
He suddenly felt light
And his spirits soared.

And he thought he saw rainbows
When they were climbing up,
But they were just gunfires
And lots of shells above.

And he climbed up the stairs
And he looked around
While most of them were already
Falling to the ground.

But the Captain's orders were sound-
That no man should remain behind
So he marched on to the ground
While shots rained him from all sides.

Many fell down,
But the rest still carried on,
Crossing the no man's land,
To the enemy's ground beyond.

But every step they took,
Their number lessened by a few.
And still he walked on,
Too numb to comprehend the view.

And then there was a sharp pain!
His blood splattered everywhere!
There was ringing in his ears.
The light seemed to disappear.

He gagged for breath,
But no voice came out.
The bullet lodged securely within,
While others ran about.

And no one noticed him.
No one seemed to care.
They were all busy falling down,
As bullets pierced them everywhere.

He saw his home,
And his smiling mother's face.
When the last traces of life,
Was beginning to fade.

Some of the bodies fell on top of him
And choked him of air.
The battlefield turned crimson,
As very few were left to move ahead.

And he did not feel proud
Nor the glory of a martyr.
He felt only regret,
For his parents' suffering.

And no more will he see the flowers
Blossoming in spring.
And no more will he see the autumn leaves
Obscuring the greens.

His cartridge was untouched,
All bullets at its place.
While his body was ravaged
With holes everywhere.

As he closed his eyes forever,
He knew he bore his burdens well,
Demanded the gods to grant him heaven
He had done his time in hell.

Pink Despair

Pink dawn now my flower paints,
A lone ranger on the dying foliage.
Shifting, fighting, for a drop of sunshine-
But instead the light, smokes its petals.
Too bright to sustain life.
Too hot to moisten a cloud.
Too raging to look behind,
The destruction that now colours the ground.
Oh my pink dawn,
I hope you give up.
For watching you futilely everyday,
Drives me magnetically
To nihilistic ways.
And makes me-
A reforming failure,
A Nightmare.

Belong

I give up my life,
To set you free.
You say you can't go on,
As long as you have me.
You say that I haunt, both
Your reality and your dreams,
And each time my memory
Makes you numb to your needs.

Don't think so much dear,
I am leaving you!
I had wished for clear skies
And the rainbows too.
But now that I've realised,
I've only darkened them for you,
Don't bother about me dear,
For I'm not bothering about you.

It seems loving and leaving
Are so easy to do!
It's so easy to give up things.
So easy to forget you.
It's so easy to go on living,
As if nothing happened between me and you.
I'm so sick of your "easy" ways,
For the last time, I'm releasing you.

I don't know anymore,
What is right or wrong.
I don't know if it,
Makes me weak or strong.
You say you want to know,
What it feels like to belong!
But how can you belong dear?
When it's you, you are running away from.

So I'm giving up my life,
To help you "belong".
There are times I wish,
I know what is going on!
There are times I hope,
I know where I'm coming from.
But all these matter no more,
Now that you are finally moving on.

Mad

Who says madness can't be a virtue?
I'm at my happiest when the crazies grip me.
Free from judgement, as they fail to pervade me.
Free from persecution, as I'm lost within me.
All the things in this life that I wanted but could not keep.
All the dreams that I had but failed to fulfil.
It's the madness in my head which keeps them apart from me.
It's the madness in my head which makes sure they never leave.
So when I am, inside my addled, troubled, mind;
The dreams are fulfilled, and the dreams are left behind.
All of existence becomes a two-sided coin.
Who said madness can't be divine?
I'm happiest and saddest when my mind is no more mine.

Free

I travelled the whole world,
And what did I find?
The world is empty,
If you are not mine.
For the days have no meaning,
Without your voice.
And the nights are a menace,
Hopeless and unkind.

I travelled the whole world,
But I had to face the truth.
That no matter how much I tried,
I could never replace you.
For you've left a void,
So big in my heart;
That to go on living
Becomes difficult on my part.

And I'm roaming and wandering,
And travelling some more.
Though I avoid all the roads,
I had walked with you before.
And trying to shake off
Your memory from my soul.
And fighting to not come
Knocking at your door.

This much I've realised,
This much I've come to see;
As long as I love you,
I can never ever be free.
And as long as I live,
Your memory will haunt me;
I can never find what others do,
My world will always be empty.

So I'm roaming and wandering,
And travelling some more.
Till I reach a place where,
Your memory won't haunt me anymore.
And if I can, I will,
Find me a new song.
So that when I leave,
I won't be defined by the one you own.

My Angel Are You There?

Do you call
With voices
Which can't be heard?
Do you call
To warn
When I'm at a loss with my world?
Do you try
To give a sign
Which means you are here?
Do you try
To comfort me
When my eyes cloud with tears?
Do you make
An effort
To get close to me?
Do you make
An effort
To try to make me see?
Do you feel
When I feel
The myriad of emotions that govern me?
Do you feel
When my fears
Cripple me from within and consume me?

Do you care
At all
When I'm too close to the edge?
Do you care
At all
When I lose my faith and break?
When I fall and fall
Do you try to prevent it?
When I suffer and suffer
Do you try to save me?
When I fail to keep my promise,
When I fail to keep up the fight,
When my world crumbles from within,
When I can't make up my mind.
When I fail to live up to my expectations,
When I'm forced to live in shame,
Do you really give a damn?
Are you even there?

Mechanical Chemical

Get my brain a fix,
It's been feeling too low lately;
Get my eyes a glass,
It's been staring too much lately.

All the blankness that my brain reads,
And all the nothingness my eyes see,
I need a glass to make them bright,
I need a fix to set them alright.

Give my heart a drag,
It's been feeling too much lately;
Give my mind a high,
It's been wallowing a bit lately.

All the chemicals that buzz around within my body,
Have aligned themselves to a new reality,
And every wisdom has moved itself out of sight,
I need something so much to set them right.

Get me a hit soon,
My blood is calling for its taste;
Get me a drink soon,
My regrets are crying to be left at its place.

It has become my soul, it has become my life.
I don't care anymore for the world outside.
All their useless talks, and their useless lies!
All their fake loves, and their ugly smiles!

For my brain breaks, and my heart aches;
And my eyes only see you, I need a hit to fade!
And my soul bleeds, and my body seethes;
My mind stores pictures of you, get me a drug for this defeat!

Put all the chemicals at its right place.
Put the regrets inside my heart, and the mask at my face.
Keep that sweet mercy glued into my vein,
And the sweet pain always hidden inside my brain.

For my mind breaks, and my soul aches;
And everywhere I look I only see your face!
I can't take anymore of this disgrace,
I need to lose myself, I need to vanish without a trace.

My Friend

In the far corner
Of this hellhole;
Where the earth runs stale
And the worms feed off;
Lies my dear friend
Of sixteen years;
His face blown open
From ear to ear.
In the morning at seven,
When the bombs hit off;
A shrapnel pierced him,
And in a moment he was gone!
How sudden the life force
Leaves the battered body!
How fast you are transformed
From a "Hero" to "nobody".
Just last night we were joking,
That the Serge laughs like a raccoon,
And now, even before the battle's begun,
My friend neither smiles or moves.
So many years together
The world as our playground.
So many happy hours

As lords of our hometown.
Now my friend lies here,
So still, so broken.
His ribs bared, his face torn,
His lungs punctured and open.

Restless

I had options waiting out for me,
Like nebulas in distant skies;
But I own a restless heart,
So I let them all go by.
My selfish soul had shrunk,
Every flittering hope hereby,
Like embers in dead white snow,
My coldness had them all die.
I could open up and give you an ocean,
If only I could know how;
For the restless heart I am,
Everything stays gone somehow.
It's that time of year again,
When people come out in throes;
Play all different acts of snobbery,
They can conjure in a day or so.
We could have been like them, you know,
Pretended to have it all.
But my restless heart would not permit me,
I had rather be alone, every fall.
So all the nebulas that once-
Danced in the fringes of my universe,
Have all left to glitter in some other expanse,
Running from the black hole that is my heart.
And in the fickle gloom,

Of the fleeting hours of morning sun,
I sometimes wish for a stable heart,
To finally make a right turn.
But I can't stand the monotony,
Of a calm waveless dead ocean;
I crave for tides and storms and tempests,
So my heart stays as restless as it can be.

Smile

Sunlight on the shore,
A gnawed silver door;
Sunlight on the staircase,
Stray tulips scattered on the floor.
A golden angel gleams,
His lips twisted in a nasty grin;
Must be feeling a king,
Watching the world dance to its whims.
Now the evening barges in,
The tulips shrink and sink,
The wind carries them to the shore,
But the water can give them life no more.
As the sun slowly fades,
The golden angel's superb head,
Now alight with a red glow
Shines brighter than before.
But his nasty smile pervades,
And amidst the darkness of the shade,
His beauty unfathomable,
Seemed to be carved from the fires of Hell.
But behold his smile!
Such wantonness beguiled,
With all the secrets under the skies,
All the deception and sweet disguise,
Is etched in that one sweet smile.

Love Me One Last Time

Love me one last time
I swear I'll change
I'll be a better person
I will make amends

Love me one last time
I swear I will cope
Give up all my bad habits
Face everything on my own

Love me one last time
I swear I won't ignore
I won't take things for granted
I won't fear the unknown

Love me one last time
I swear I will try
I will find a meaning
And never hide behind lies

Love me one last time
I swear I'll have faith
I'll face the storm head on
Won't cower and wait for death

Love me one last time
I swear this will be the last
I will make a new beginning
I'll make up for my past

Love me for the last time
Don't make me stay the same
If you leave now I'll break
So save me from myself

Other Worlds Other Thoughts

When I close my eyes forever
Let it be on a rainy day,
When I breath my last
Let the morning slowly fade,
And when I can feel no more
Let the rain fall on my face,
And when the raindrops bathe my body
At that very moment help me disappear.

I don't want to be an entity of this world
I'll just be a part of the clouds floating above,
Watching the Universe through the eyes of God
The world below me no more my concern,
I long for the day when golden skies gleam
And I become the rain and fall on the autumn leaves,
And I merge with the dust, the dust of the Earth
And evaporate and rise up again to the skies above.

Endless

Years will come and pass off in the shadows,
Ages will come and set forth its ruins,
But you and I will remain.
Remain till there are ages no more,
Till there are worlds no more,
Till there is no time or it's shadow.
It is the Music in our souls!
This music that keeps us so.
That plays out through the ruins of time,
Unites us back every time.
Each time to utter the same verse,
Each time to lay the same chords,
Though in a different tune,
And in different words.
Many ages will come and go,
Many moments shall write their tales,
But you and I shall come back again,
The same melody ruling our fates.
You and I will remain…
When there is nothing more but dust of this world,
When even dust will rule itself to emptiness,
You and I shall remain my friend,
Forever a light in this eternal darkness.

Things That Plague My Mind

The scatter of light in the dancing shadows,
My stillwater heart with the embers of unearthly sorrows,
These are the things that now plague my mind,
Every circumstance just further burdens my plight.
Lights and flames and a thousand icicles,
Lodge together in my mind for acceptance,
And I, petrified, unable to make a choice,
Unable to give meaning to my fruitless voice,
Wither and quiver in the departing daylight,
Merging with the darkness of,
All the things that plague my mind.

Bewitched

I look at your eyes
I'm lost in there
The world seems to be fading
Slowly fading away.
I look at your face
And my heart skips a beat
The world seems to be slipping
Slipping away to retreat.
I look at this moment
And I feel unreal
That this is just a fantasy
And I'm not really here.
And all the stars
That could ever shine
With you here
All of them go out of sight.
Everything becomes stagnant
Lost in time
You bewitch me
Body, soul and mind.
I look at your lips
I'm fading in there
You are a trip to

Heaven, Hell and everywhere.
Someone wake me up
From my dream here
I'm lost inside some reality
And I'm starting to belong there.

I Just Left

I left that country, I left that place,
I left everyone without a trace,
Some say I left to find myself,
But let's not get ahead of ourselves,
I left because I just don't care.

Don't look for me anymore here,
For you might find what you don't like,
And don't look for me in this place again,
For believe me I've left nothing behind.

I left that country, I left that place,
I left everyone without a trace,
They say I left to kill the pain,
But let's not get ahead of ourselves,
I left because I simply don't care.

Don't let them think I left for love,
For you know I'm not that foolish,
And don't let them think I left for you,
For you know I'm as fickle as the wind.

I left because I do not care,
If this place changes or rots in hell,
If the people sink or just float away,
If they go on living or just drops down dead,
I left because I just don't care.

So don't feel bad, it's not your fault babe,
I'm just not the one that you so craved,
Don't fool yourself thinking that maybe I cared,
For you know it's not in my nature to share.

For I'm no more there, I've left that place,
I've left them all without a trace,
They believed I left to be myself,
But let's not get ahead of ourselves,
I left because I simply don't care.

Don't light those candles, I was never that brave,
Don't keep my memory, erase whatever I've said,
Don't try to forgive, just try to forget,
For I'm content to be the one that got away.

Cold

Please don't make me feel cold
I can see you dancing on the threshold
Please don't make me feel cold
Stop the pain from this stronghold
Give me something stronger than the one before.

The pills don't affect me anymore
Pain has gripped me on a death choke
Please don't make me feel cold
The drugs they warm me no more.

I can see you fading outside
All the love I hold crumbles inside
Please don't make me feel cold tonight
Without the drugs it's so hard to hide
Give me something let me take a flight.

If the heavens do shatter tonight
I'll fade with it like a summer sigh
All the blood's been boiled and turned to ice
Just let me be warm for this one night.

Please don't make me feel so cold
Oh, the meds they calm me no more
Pain like ice crawls up my soul
Please don't make me cold anymore
Give me something stronger than the one before.

Depth

I will walk down the edges of blue waters
Where the white waves float the sand within my toes
I will see the sun sink beneath the ocean
And feel the moonlight dancing on the shores.

I will think nothing, do nothing and be nothing
While the night grows old
The smell of the ocean will soothe my nostrils
And my brain will open up a new door.

And when that door opens,
the world will close for me
I'll be merging, merging, merging
within the depths of the sea
No words or thoughts
can then overcome me
On reaching the floor of the ocean
I will reach eternity.

Cry

Am I to sink beneath the sands?
Or am I to swim the arduous shores?
To see once more the vision I had lost,
To feel the world through the eyes of my soul.
Should I maintain more lies?
Should I fake more love?
Should I go on breaking hearts?
And wading through the whole town's blood?
Or should I just give myself up?
Corrode the dreams with the acid of my wrath?
Surrender my sanity to unbridled chaos,
And let nothingness before fade to nothingness beyond?

Futile

I seethe-
Not from anger
But the lack of it!
From the constant shallowness
Of perpetual hope;
But never fulfilment-
Which plagues me.

I soar-
Not from excitement
But the lack of it;
Nooks and crannies-
For the wings of escape
To come find me and
Make me hollow no more.

And here I am
The wind still barges on
And I march and rage
And kick and ache
And no oasis
Just oceans of sand around.

Decay

The last tear on your forgetful face,
Runs down like a battled loser -
the last of its race
And darkness
self-imposed and hostile
Creeps inside and roams
like worms feeding on flesh.

Tinted skies
and harrowed moods
A restless caricature
now stands on the
place of once knightly saint.

Did you count?
As pieces of your soul deserted you.
Like cowardly soldiers
at the sign of approaching doom;
one by one leaving
your overwhelmed consciousness;
like wilting flower petals.
While turning you to stone.

Have you noticed?
The mirror no more showing your lines.
But accusingly beseeching you
to dissect its hollow insides;
and your image shifts.
Like ripples on a breezy lake.
And fixes on the picture
of what you've made of yourself.

Tell me does it shatter?
And you hear the shards
pierce your brain;
while you smile coyly.
And your mouth lies beauty
and your eyes stain austere.
But your mind - bleeds.
The shards get stuck and
it's hard to remove them from within.

But no they do not see.
They can never know.
How you stare longingly
at the ground eleven storeys below.
With the smile plastered on your face,
your shining teeth blazing,
your air of suavity
and your mirth
forever deceiving,
fails to reach
behind your pretty eyes,
and unearth the ugliness
that you've decorated inside.

Until it's too late!
Too late to peel off your skin
for your insides
have huddled out.
Too corroded to fit in.
Now they have unleashed
the battery of long years.
To feast on your outsides
as nothing is left to eat within.

The smile now gone.
The eyes now dead.
The mirror now cracked.
The worms now fed.

I Will Return: The Warrior's Ballad

Your song on my lips
Your name in my heart
I sail the seven seas
Away from your world
Battles await me
My nation falls
The shadow lingers
Fear pervades all
I battle for the light
For the freedom of the race
But all the while my eyes
Search for your face
You give me hope
When my strength fails
Your face springs light
When my faith breaks
With my forces outnumbered
Darkness engulfing my land
Few warriors stand to defend
The nation which once was grand
When despair grips me
For the fate is only a cage
I long to return to you

Our promise gives me strength
For though we are apart
And my fight wages on
Keep your faith on me
And I will return
When my duty is done
And this darkness gone
I will come back for you
I will return

Fortitude

The soul wants more than just the soul
The soul wants to break these shallow walls
The soul wants to crash like breaking wave
The soul wants more, more than it can take
It is not in its nature to remain content
It is not in its nature to calm its urges
For the soul like the Universe wants to expand
The soul wants to break whatever limits it can
It is not natural to lock the soul in a cage
To stop feeding its fantasies, to curb its rage
For like a swollen ocean that dances at the storm
The soul can't be contained, can't be conformed
The soul wants to rage, the soul wants to storm
The soul wants to unfurl all the passions it can summon
The soul wants to wreak havoc at all barriers it sees
The soul will always triumph in its efforts to be free
It is not in its nature to be linked up in chains
To pine, to cower, to wither and wilt in shame
For when it will shatter, it will dance in flames
It is futile to pacify it, to train it to be a slave
For the soul longs more than just the soul
The soul longs more than just to feel whole

The soul wants more than even salvation and divine joy
The soul wants to be rid of all efforts to keep it coy
The soul wants to be free
To go to places no one had been
To be limitless with abandoned glee
The soul wants to be free…

Empty

All your vanity and your plainness
All the miles that lead to your doorstep
All that I had crossed to reach the centre of your heart
I should have just let the moments to depart.
For everything now is tainted by your love
And to behold it requires strength I just don't have
The voices that torment me, every night I summon
They comfort me more than all your memories I had known.
I walk through the town directionless and distraught
All the houses look same and all the faces are dark
I long to find a house empty enough for me
But too many memories surround and suffocate me.
I don't even want you, or the glories I'm supposed to find
I don't even need certainty to placate my troubled mind
I don't even care about you or your words or your smile
I don't even know anymore which life is mine.
I long just for a space where I can be free
A space empty enough and full enough for me
Where life, time, mind, soul and you can never find me
And I can be free of the lepers that leech around me.
I just want to be empty, I just want to be free
Tell the voices to go, tell your memories to leave me

Tell the music to stop, tell the dreams to forsake me
Tell every fantasy to surrender and abandon me.
I don't want the dreams, I don't want the truths
I don't want the luxuries that used to paralyse me
I just want to be empty, empty enough to be free
I just long to be empty, empty enough to be me.

Frenzy

How I have loved you
I do not know.
Through desperation unquenchable
always thirsting for more.
On nights when the red stars
shimmer in the distance
so does my soul shiver for
a breath of your presence.

How I have longed for you
I do not know.
Like a madman runs amok
desperate for a clean window.
On restless time I had danced away
my waiting, for your green eyes.
And you unable to break away
from the censorship of hollow time,
have left me like a withering rose
helplessly watching its petals fly.

How I could just watch you
and let everything else depart,
Your pale green eyes
and my red aching heart,
All the bits and pieces
in the moments, scattered.
Nothing, absolutely nothing
ever made to last.

How I've dreamed about you
I do not know.
Like ripples than dances in lakes
searching for a shore.
Like fireflies that cease to be
at the break of dawn,
I have dreamed of you
forever and forever long.
But like petals that glaze
the sultry summer air,
you move apart from me
slowly and slowly away.
How I long to be
completely yours.
Push away all of
existence into chaos.
Merge into your soul
and finally find heaven.

There is a holiness in
loving someone this way.
Petals in the wind and
your blinking green eyes,
If one day I could be yours
I'd let it all fly.

Love

Is love the colour of a painter's delight?
Or the madness of a schizophrenic's eye?
A chaos on the brink of rupture,
Like overwrought cloudy skies
on a stormy morning?
Or a sigh of the woods, at the loss
of its leaves to winter dawn?
Some have praised it,
Some have paled it,
Some have consumed it,
Some have failed it.
But never a fellow,
Past or present,
Have ever owned it.
For in the end as they all say-
Love "wins".
It succeeds in-
Ripping your hearts,
Robbing your brains,
Blinding your sights,
And you're a fool again!
Words of longing and pain
have built up a mountain.
"Broken hearts" have immortalised
a thousand starchy pamphlets.

There standing in the cold rain,
the clown's heart bleeds,
while his smile spreads.
Numbed by love's caprices,
yet yearning for the same.
No wisdom or insight into the
machinations of the mind.
Sees the world through the
blindness of love-soaked eyes.
Fails to understand the basic fact of life-
that 'love' doesn't exist in selfish humankind.
It's Security, mankind seeks.
It's Stability, his right brain needs.
It's Scarcity, for which he makes war.
It's Sanctity, his heart yearns for.
'Love' should be left to the Sun and Stars.

Lies

Tell my lies to go someplace new
My brain's been overflowing with them few
One of these days it will burst through
And give way to ugliness long due
Tell my lies to find some other brain to chew
Tell them to invade somebody new
Tell my lies to stop lying so much
It's been too long, it's been enough
Sometimes truth is needed to still a battered heart
Tell my lies to stop tearing me apart
Tell my lies to stop infesting my tongue
Drive them away for I'm finally done
My lies have come undone!
My lies have come undone!
No raging hell but a slow agonising burn
My lies, they have all come undone.

The Difference of a Night

Tomorrow the ravens will come for my flesh,
What can I say, this is the martyr's end,
This is what goes through within my mind's eye,
For come morning, and I will possibly die.
And as I lie down and watch the night stars,
I think and think, but I fail to understand,
How can a night as beautiful as this,
Give birth to a morning that can rival hell's pit.
But fates, there are none, when you need them for you,
They only manifest for the fortunate few,
But those of us, who toil by the night,
Bear the burden of the enemy's might,
Can expect no miracles from the Gods' fickle minds,
But only bullets and shells and more missiles.
The Moon, it tugs at the clutches of my heart,
Forces me to remember the times before the war,
Where I lay down under it and sang its melody,
Now here I am under the same, waiting for death to take me.
For I'm no fool, I know how the world works,
There is no glory just a sickening sense of loss,
There are horrors and blood clots and pieces of broken bones,
But no, there is no glory, no glory in it anymore.
So today is my last night with the fragrance in the air,
Tomorrow at dawn, there'll be nothing but poison everywhere.

Distance

Do you think about me,
in strange afternoons?
Like I do about you,
at the height of my blues?
Like me, do you then sigh?
As wishes turn to nothing
and slowly die.
Do you feel the vacuum
that tugs at your heart?
And it feels suffocating
to even utter a word!
Am I always on your mind?
Like you are in mine?
Or am I just a fleeting cloud
never to colour your sky?
Do you wish like I do?
To resolve the distance
that divides me from you?
For I dream everyday about
no distance between us.
I dream everyday that
my mind and heart are one.

I dream everyday that
I am joined with your mind.
And am finally, utterly,
completely divine.

The Warrior and The Traitor

Fallen to the ground
Without a sound
Still like a lake
Is he sleeping or is he dead?
While all hell breaks loose
And you are left to choose
Whether to kill or be killed
When you know it won't change anything
And you ask too late
The question about your fate
What exactly did you gain?
For you know you are no saint
You have liberated no one
You have achieved nothing
You are just a pawn in the game
Of the people who belong to no country
All they want is money
Bearing their name
And their deluded projection
Of glory and fame
And so you fight
The wars they create
And you go to your hell
For the sins they make
So now you have a gun

And there's nowhere you can run
You try to clear your voice
In war it's hard to make a choice
If you choose to kill
They will brand you a murderer
And if you do not
You will be charged as a traitor

Slow Decay of a Burned Heart

I have blundered!
Like a fool, my pride had taken me.
Like a fool I thought everything can be mechanised.
But the heart wants what the heart wants.
No plotting of this Universe can make a heart stop!
Thought I could tame my fiery soul!
What a fool!
I'd rather burn!!
Than tame it to placation.
Reduced to a mere cog!
In this endless dance of the fortunes-
I'd rather burn!!
My vanity betook me for a fool!
And now my untamed, unhinged soul,
Has claimed vengeance!
If only I had the strength of good sense.
Now ride! Foolish heart,
This funeral of your making.
Where happiness and exhilaration are buried.
And monotony reigns supreme!
Ride this momentous foolishness!
To the point of suffocation.
Till purgatory traps you and frees you to decay.